HIDE NOW

Glyn Maxwell has won several awards for his poetry, including the Somerset Maugham Prize, the E. M. Forster Prize from the American Academy of Arts and Letters and the Geoffrey Faber Memorial Prize. His work has been shortlisted for the Whitbread, Forward and T. S. Eliot Prizes. Many of his plays have been staged in the UK and USA, including *The Lifeblood*, which won British Theatre Guide's 'Best Play' Award at the Edinburgh Fringe in 2004, and *Liberty*, which premiered at Shakespeare's Globe in 2008.

ALSO BY GLYN MAXWELL

Poetry

Tale of the Mayor's Son
Out of the Rain
Rest for the Wicked
The Breakage
The Boys at Twilight: Poems 1990–95
Time's Fool
The Nerve
The Sugar Mile

Plays

Plays One: The Lifeblood, Wolfpit, The Only Girl
   in the World
Plays Two: Broken Journey, Best Man Speech,
   The Last Valentine
The Forever Waltz
Liberty

HIDE NOW

Glyn Maxwell

PICADOR

First published 2008 by Picador
an imprint of Pan Macmillan Ltd
Pan Macmillan, 20 New Wharf Road, London N1 9RR
Basingstoke and Oxford
Associated companies throughout the world
www.panmacmillan.com

ISBN 978-0-330-45624-1

9 8 7 6 5 4 3 2 1

A CIP catalogue record for this book is available from
the British Library.

Printed and bound in the UK by
CPI Mackays, Chatham ME5 8TD

for Alfie Rose Maxwell

Contents

Acknowledgements

Acknowledgements are due to the editors of the following publications in which some of these poems (or versions of them) first appeared: 'Ariadne to Theseus' was first published in *Agenda*; 'Catworld' (as 'Fundamentalism') in *Fulcrum*; 'Hometown Mystery Cycle' in the *Guardian*; 'The Old Lad' in the *London Review of Books*; 'Contours of Fall' in *Metre*; 'All Things Bright', 'Country Birthday' and 'It Too Remains' in the *New Criterion*; 'The Shivers' in the *New Republic*; 'Element It Has' in the *New Yorker*; 'Mandelstam' in the *New York Sun*; 'Dust and Flowers' in *Open City*; 'Dream-I-Believe' and 'Fire Came' in the *Paris Review*; 'Anything But the Case' and 'Old Smile at the Roast' in *Poetry*; 'Flags and Candles' and 'Kaspar Hauser' in *Poetry Review*; 'Empire State', 'One Thousand Nights and Counting', 'Thinking: *Earth*', 'The Tinsel Man' and 'A Walk by the Neva' in the *Times Literary Supplement*.

'Ariadne to Theseus' was written as a libretto for the composer Elena Langer, and performed (as *Ariadne*) at the Almeida Opera Festival in 2003. 'Number Three', 'Long Journey', 'Lit Windows' and 'Thinking: *Earth*' were all written for the BBC World Service programme *Thinking Earth*, broadcast in 2004: versions of them were published in the chapbook *Handside Lane*.

The Old Lad

I close my eyes and see them waving cloths they found.
Rags and things a thousand feet above the ground.

Making calls they made and saying words they said.
Here comes a girl in red to be the girl in red.

There go the men in shirts. I will not focus in
on any face again and, as I focus in,

arms stretch out as if *There goes the superstar!*
I go on trying for years to not know who they are.

Looked for ways to cope with coping with this shit.
Woke up at four, damned if I hadn't hit on it.

Smiled about it, thing my skull has always done.
United with the old lad, sang in unison.

Felt the soft foam falling from a rigid prow,
gainsaying all there is: *Now don't you worry now.*

Couldn't believe I'd cracked it, like the wide-eyed folk
who think all strangers function as a spy-network

making the stuff that makes the papers. Smiled a smile
beyond belief in presidential-spokesman style.

Ran back and forth a century from ape to ape
to seek what's *not* okay by so sincere a gape . . .

Okay the neighbour's starving and okay he's here.
Okay a billion times the bit we gave last year

let's funnel into rubbish-bags and tie the ties.
Okay the trains are pulling out and full of eyes.

Okay to sport a badge, okay to wave a cloth.
Okay some went forever and some won't sod off.

Okay the ones like Cheney, whom you mustn't name
and spoil the poem, do the motherfucking same

as ever, and okay the poles to north and south
are vowels: meat and drink and sex to the one mouth

of the only lad, no worries. It is not a smile
that makes you ache. It won't be over in a while

like mine, but I keep trying. Here it comes again,
and now I'm going to die one day and don't care when,

why, with whom, or who remembers what I did.
The smile is wide and smaller only than the lid.

Do it in turbulence as well, I'm a total mess,
but beaming like a stewardess at the stewardess,

who learned to do it years ago from her old bones,
and can do it hissing info into hidden phones

when the time comes. I fly the blue Atlantic sky
in my last century and yours and by and by

my eyes are holes, my heart is air, my knuckles shine.
Only God controls the Fasten Seat Belt sign.

It's all He does. I turn a frail page of grey
and all the news that's fit to print this Saturday

is printed there this Saturday. The news that's not,
the old lad's grinning over in a book he's got.

He's pointing out what's funny and it's everything.
We're starting our descent and I am done with him.

Flags and Candles

Flags line up an hour before they're chosen,
wave back along the row at others like them.
Candles sit in boxes or lie still,

sealed, and each imagines what will happen.
Flags will not accept the explanation
of why they were not needed as they are now.

Candles feel they're made of stuff that's soft
for a good cause, though maybe not their own cause.
Tall flags love all flags if it's their flags.

Small flags are okay about immense flags.
Candles doze in xylophones of colour,
thrilled their purpose may be merely pattern.

Flags are picked out one by one. The others
muster in the gap and say *Gap, what gap?*
Candles dream of something that will change them,

that is the making of and death of candles.
Flags don't dream of anything but more flags.
The wind is blowing; only the landscape changes.

Candles have the ghost of an idea
exactly what the wick is for: they hope so.
Flags have learned you can't see flags at nighttime,

no way, not even giants in a windstorm.
Candles learn that they may do their damnedest
and go unnoticed even by old candles.

When I wave flags, flags think it's the world waving
while flags are holding fast. When I light candles,
candles hold the breath that if it came

would kill them; then we tremble like our shadows.
Flags know nothing but they thump all morning.
Candles shed a light and burn to darkness.

A Play of the Word

Something was done and she ran from a town
and I'm glad it was done or she wouldn't have come,
but she wouldn't have gone and she's long gone now,
so I'm wondering why and remembering how.

Her hair was the various colours of leaves
in the fall in a heap as we watched her asleep
and we stood there like words with the ink still wet,
as reminders of something she'd likely forget,

or read in the morning and scrunch in a ball.
Her eyes were so wide that they had a seaside
and a faraway sail in one eye then the other
till I envied my brother and I've not got a brother.

Her mouth had this shape that it made and you can't,
we tried it all week and our lower lips ached
as we pointed this out and she didn't know how
she was doing it. I'm sort of doing it now.

Her hands were so delicate delicate things
were careful with them and the length of her arm
was an hour when I saw it at rest on a sill
with a twig in its hand that's in my hand still.

Her body was everything nobody knew
and discussed in the dark till it wasn't that dark
but her feet were so callused they made it clear
We two will be getting her out of here.

Something was done and she ran from a town
and I'm glad it was done or she wouldn't have come,
but she wouldn't have gone and she's long gone now,
so I'm wondering why and remembering how.

You all have your tales and we too have a tale
in the form of a play that we stage in the day,
it's a play of the Lord, it's a play of the Word:
if it had to be written it has to be heard.

And we opened the barn for the costumes and sets
that have always been there and the dust on the air
would set us all sneezing and telling old jokes
of old times and old shows in old years with old folks.

And one was the Maker and one was the Man,
and one was the Angel and one was the Stranger,
and all the old lines were as fresh as cold beer
in a morning in March in that field over there.

But she was so puzzled her mouth did that thing
and her eyes were a mist and her hand was a fist
that she held to her chin till our play was complete.
Then she started to laugh. She was right by that gate.

It isn't for laughter we play in our show.
It's not at all funny. It isn't for money,
it isn't for love. But she laughed and her eyes
were the fog as it shrugs in the face of sunrise,

and her ribs were the sea in the shirt she wore:
we were sickened to follow its suck and its swell,
she was out of our reach, she had always been,
but that was our choice, if you see what I mean.

Something was done and she ran from a town
and I'm glad it was done or she wouldn't have come,
but she wouldn't have gone and she's long gone now,
so I'm wondering why and remembering how.

Why are you laughing, we wanted to say,
till one of us did and we wanted to hide,
and her glistening eyes had no answer to that,
so we waited like birds for her swallowing throat

to be still and it was, and she stared at the ground
like a book of her own to be counted upon.
Everything here is made out of card.
Take light from the World and you're left with the Word

which she seemed to be trying to show in the dust
as we crowded to see and could never agree
what she said after that – that our Maker was sick
of his Word? That our souls could be drawn with a stick?

That our Man was a rainbow, our Angel should hang?
Or the other way round? But whichever way round
there was nothing to do but the next thing we did,
which was take it in turns to repeat what she said

having tiptoed unnoticed away on our own
to the elders and olders who had to be told
what a creature she was and how little she knew
and how hard she was laughing and what we should do.

But I was among the ones crowding her light
so her shadow was gone but I wasn't the one
who asked her to tell us what *should* have been done,
in a voice with arms folded and uniform on.

Something was done and she ran from a town
and I'm glad it was done or she wouldn't have come,
but she wouldn't have gone and she's long gone now,
so I'm wondering why and remembering how.

And he asked her to say what the Maker *would* say
and a few ran away. I did not run away
but I want to have done, so I sit on this gate
where there's nothing to wait for at all and I wait.

And she looked at who'd said it and looked at who'd not
and she stood and she started to speak from her heart
what the Maker would say. I can say this to you.
For who lives in this shell of a town but we two?

The elders assembled like stones in a boat
but it sailed as it could, while it could, when it could,
and then I saw nothing and now I see all
and I wait and there's nothing to wait for at all.

And the wind caught the fire with the last of its strength,
the fire they began for what had to be done,
but the fire caught the town and it burned in my eyes
till my eyes were the desert an hour from sunrise.

And I talk of we two, but it's me on this gate,
with an echo of wind when the song has an end,
but the wind didn't do what I too didn't do,
and we won't breathe a word till there's reason to.

Forty Forty

History covered its eyes and counted the way
    kids count: getting faster
then slowing to halves, quarters, sixteenths
    but nonetheless faster,

faster in words but slower and slower to reach
    like Zeno's arrow,
though finally all the way to some fat figure
    ending in zero.

Then History turned and blinked: right there
    stood a boy by a hedgerow,
holding his hands to his eyes and saying
    I'm coming to get you!

And his confidence in a game he had
    quite misunderstood
was awful to see and if History didn't correct him
    others would,

so History ventured slowly towards him
    and – I don't know how –
very gently took little hands in big hands and said
    hide now.

Dream-I-Believe

Dream-I-Believe I brought
   out of the night still streaming
      out *It was real I was right!*

Dream present still I could still
   believe in, if I twisted
      likelihood to serve it . . .

Dream that was gone I mourned
   and quoted, sought and lingered
      on sections to my liking.

Dream I had had depended
   on puns, events, encounters
      even to come to mind now.

I seemed to have held four faiths
   by breakfast, and I'd packed them
      fighting to their buses.

So I could sit exhausted,
   stretching in the sunbeams
      like my mother in the old days.

Cassandra Tells Fortunes

The water-jug let fall – a blink of hope –
it shattering.
Liquid steals away, the fragments rock
themselves to sleep.
Slaves mop up around me and I still
tell fortunes.

I tell them to the King who makes his finger
draw quick rings
in air to say *Go on go on go on*
to the section
where I love you! (listen all you crocks of shit
to this bit . . .)

I tell them to the General whose days
are spent in battle,
who looks affronted even to be seated,
that I see nothing
but curtains, soon, and he stares at me like I'm
on something.

I tell them to the soldier who'll be back
before he knows it.
His private hope about me has consumed him
and perches there.
He will perish far from home. He says *You mean*
on honeymoon!

I tell them to the sweethearts, I tell two,
or begin to,
but they say *Tell ours together if you please!*
I don't say I
can't see that, I just close my eyes and soon
there's no one.

And I tell them to my gaoler when there's no one,
who feeds me
figs he stole and because he has a future
without feature
there's little to say, but he pours my lemon-water
so carefully.

Kaspar Hauser

My dream of her
was memories in heaps and the whole morning
at her age now

I think of her
is memories in heaps. In the great daylight
I do nothing

but see stars
like the wolf-boy they sat down in a world
of nonsense.

Empire State

Departed I could see her
from my new room in Manhattan,
lonely among letters
in the tallest word in English.

It's like she'd crept alongside,
a great bejewelled someone
at the dark edge of a party
we could not stand any longer.

And still at the wide window
we considered making contact,
she haplessly three-coloured
and I knowing all about that,

but we settled for the vista
through the traffic to the water.
Since *nothing lasts forever*
was about all I could muster.

Ariadne to Theseus

after Ovid, Heroides X

As white as the white page before there falls
the print of loss, so were the sheets I rose
to find this morning, and the roar of shells
    was all my voice,
        Theseus.

Sleep went below the visible horizon
and the moon was stranded. On the trackless shore
I echoed every rock that told me *Gone* . . .
    My tangled hair,
        Theseus,

was a labyrinth abandoned to the dark.
And the first letter of this far lament
was A on the sea, the separating ache
    of a sail. The wind,
        Theseus,

lit up my eyes like candles, and like flame
I stood, I was blown back, I rose again.
The waves crept up, they left behind your name
    spelt on the sand –
        THESEUS –

as if a sign on the eroded scrolls
of a lost tribe, as if it were the reason
nothing came to pass. I climb the hills.
    Now the horizon,
        Theseus,

is all I see: a line that forms a ring
below the sky. Its only sound is O.
What horrors prowl that circle? There's no string
    for me to follow,
        Theseus,

out of such a place. Only to go
from all the world — you went from all of mine —
I dream of. A kept vow, a broken vow:
    each is a chain,
        Theseus,

and through the grinding of the green salt sea
you hear me roam my island like the beast
you left for dead. I love you. Now the sky
    darkens the east,
        Theseus,

darkens the shore, shortens the little page
I beat upon, and how I meet the end
is all that's left untold, a ragged edge
    for the undersigned
        Ariadne

Love Songs from Plays

Dust and Flowers

Everyone ever was shuddering past
In a rubbishy cyclone of them and the dust
And my eyes were attempting to follow some face
I would lose in a blur like a chariot-race

So I'd try that again, and to anyone seeing
I seemed to be one who was stuck disagreeing
And shaking my head sort of slowly forever
Like somebody chronically stupid or clever,

When breaking the surface between it and me,
You stood there as quiet as Sunday will be
While we're having a Saturday – I was the same
For no time at all, till your face and your frame

Were nodding my head up and down on its stem
Like a flower in the rain at the height of a storm,
But afterwards too, like a flower in a breeze,
And always, which doesn't have flower-similes.

Anything But the Case

Do me my elegy now, or I'll scrawl the thing
I scrawl as you're going or screw in a ball when you're gone,
Or you and I write unaware in each other's tongue
That you or I ever set foot . . . Or do what our son
And/or little daughter got done: got our brilliant names
Pricily grooved in marble by one skilled
In times of loss; dream iridescent dreams
It's that first Saturday. Let this hour be filled
With anything but the case, so that Time the clerk
Goes panting in horror from gremlin to error to glitch
And his screen is stripes and he knows he saved his work
In one of a billion files but fuck knows which,
And he lets us alone or, at worst, as we tiptoe by,
Feels we're familiar, can't for the world say why.

The Deal

The trick of the day was won
so handily by the sun
when the cards spread out and shone

that the game went still for a while.
Whoever was meant to deal
would have to wait for a smile

to glitter and catch on,
soon broaden into fun,
then thoroughly be gone.

Contours of Fall

A show expected of them,
    fall trees in late September.
Maybe they dream of ugliness,
loss, discolour,

like girls of old New England
    clustered a time together
might well have done to brace themselves,
shriek in a mirror,

as the contour is approaching,
    men of miles away,
who see what comes as no surprise
rapturously,

and the trees can no more stem it
    than the girls behind the door;
all slump into the strict allure
men gallop for.

The brown they think goodwill to them,
    the red'll do for love,
the golds and ambers anything
they're short of;

so the trees turn and the girls walk
    and neither learns a colour
to make these strangers go away,
not grief, pallor,

not misery, till a stave of contours
    swings by in a breath.
One colour does for all thereafter
in the north.

Cassandra and the Night Watch

They send ahead their cackling like servants
to say they're coming. Like I heard the ocean
say a wave will break.
I'm wide awake
like you are,
tracing the glyph for *now* on my one cushion.

They burst into my cell and cry *It's us two,
witch-lady, look!* As if I caught the windstorm
saying there'll be leaves.
Between their graves
I dance
with them, they have me twirling to their anthem.

They tire like battles and they rest like cities,
blue with heat. They hiss the candles out
and grin at their burnt fingers.
I say *Sing us
the song
of what's-to-come* at the same time they say it.

They listen like a sprawling black lagoon
in the earth's last forest. They stir like it's TV.
One talks in sleep like software . . .
sometime . . . somewhere . . .
the other
staggers toward me desperate for me.

Rush

Rush of blood, reveille of the lovely,
roll-call of the long-gone: adults are pressed
into this play, as if by a determined only
child who for a morning, as the storm builds,
    must have his way.

A scene that never happened is one tale.
So is a scene that did in a deep breath
and either one begins as I exhale
all innocence. In any I play someone
    I sometimes am.

Trespass and cost-of-trespass, puerile logic
structurally sound: I admire my story
while writhing in it, I can only change it
for the better now, it skips like a bad CD
    or jams like one

so the moment trills absurdly in one place –
then all's sucked out of sight. I lie alone
in a world city. Love was to do with this
so long ago. That's what I make of what
    I kept of it.

Element It Has

It may not be the same, what we appear
to thrive or slow or fade in, though across
its white expanses steadily we stare;

the only common element it has
is loss, and it may differ in the terms
it gives it. And it thickens with the days,

thins in the night as if it more than seems
a carbon thing, afflicted, prone to what?
To us, as if obscurely hopes or harms

can come to it, as if it walks the street
in love, abashed, abused — as if it, too,
expands to wonder at the point of it —

contracts to desperation in the blue
morning, helplessly expands anew.

One Thousand Nights
and Counting

I love her stories but they're all alike.
    I don't mean that.
And I'd only dare to think it on my break
and all I get to do on that
is piss this platinum – eat your heart out Midas –
    until I'm done
and trot like only tyrants trot
quick-quick in case I miss one.

Litre or two to go. Now when I say
    they're all alike
I only mean – I mean in a good way –
that she has certain themes (I'm like
a literary prof these days!) and they,
    what's the word,
recur: Aleppo, Baghdad, Cairo,
wherever the story's set

it's all the same shebang, but this last one
    better not end,
dear, for that rosy glint on the horizon
is only something being sharpened . . .
Where was I? I was training a critic's eye
    on common themes –
as all my thunder starts to trickle –
I'm only like all storms,

all storms are just like me. Theme Number One:
    the djinn: the djinn
I love, don't get me wrong – without the djinn
you might as well read magazines,
lists! – but must they always come in jars
    and rise as smoke
so horribly I can't see any light
for one great swell of muck?

I only ask. I'm reaching for the soap.
    I can hear from here
the clearing of her little throat, the clap
of olive hands – it's just not fair
I'm who I am! I was the master here!
    I mean I am,
and anyway, I've points to make,
a Second Theme. Ahem:

the chambers underground. There are always chambers
    some innocent
tradesman goes about his day and wanders
into by some accident
and bingo, X has lost an eye, hey presto
    Y lies dead,
and treasure's everywhere, but cursed,
and stuff goes really bad –

I'm drying my hands as quickly as I can,
    dear (I call her)
but not before I mention that a man
can dream, yes, in sound and colour
dreams are free, yet, in your little tales,
    Peculiar Soul,
they all come true – the smoke comes true,
revenge in a deep hole,

men without eyes and djinn with nothing but,
    a sot who dreams
he'll rule the world and lifts it off a plate
one morning, men in dog-forms
who begged to differ, dogs in man-forms
    who knows why?
She doesn't know, she's calling me
by *name* now! What if I

just stayed here in these echoey cool halls
    forever, free
of stories, free of her, among the smells
of lavender and lime and me,
the free will of the water? That can't be,
    for who but I
can end it, when she shuts the book
at dawn and meets my eye

and I meet hers? Nobody, that's who,
    when our eyes meet
(her eyes so green) I will know what to do,
when the extraordinary book is shut
and her fingers touch each other. Till that day
    I am content
to hear her poor preposterous tales
of how the old world went.

Martial Diptych

I

By stock-still flags on the hottest day
    Recorded,
He delivered a rousing speech to about six
    Hundred.

At the end of his speech the caps would be hurled
    Skyward.
The sky was the blue of the blue sky on a
    Postcard.

There it all is in a black-and-white shot in the
    Paper,
Depicting the memorable scene at his alma
    Mater.

The sky is the grey it would turn and, in capitals
    Under:
PRESIDENT RALLIES THE TROOPS FOR THE WAR
    ON THUNDER.

II

PRESIDENT RALLIES THE TROOPS FOR THE WAR
ON WATER
I see in my scrapbook. I used to be a
Reporter.

The bleachers were pegged to the sand, and about six
Hundred
Were waiting to hurl their caps, and nobody
Wondered

Where was the ocean gone. The highest
Recorded
Temperature rose and twelve hundred hands
Applauded

Everything. I looked at the sharp
Horizon
Through twirling and falling caps and I saw it
Whiten.

Tale of the Story-of-All-Stories

Now, from above, a desert in the future
was a flattened page we knew from an old atlas.
Earth blacked out except for its heat-clusters,
stars in oil.
     Now there were only bonfires

and the charred trails towards them. Down those ruts
came stories of what happened, borne on carts,
set down in a soot-acre in the woods,
begun again
     for an oval of cocked heads,

the flies at every face no proof-of-life.
Proof-of-life was baring of red teeth
if stories failed, was catches in the breath
if breath survived
     the new ordeals of faith.

Some stories lost their nerve and just stood still,
or tried to fix one unoffending smile
on all the circle, turning like a wheel
that spins so fast
     it bores itself a hole.

Some stories lost their minds but were heard out
anyway, devoid of point or plot,
late-stage dementia reckoned to be thought,
that died as it
     was sagely nodded at.

And the opposite – a story that knew much
would talk in puzzles: cornered at a hedge
at the twelfth hour, on the wrong end of rage,
it glimpsed its face
    in a real cutting edge.

One story loved the stuff it had to wear
and was buried in it; one had need of fire
and a spangled girl it could make disappear:
when the night fell
    nobody lived there.

Stories ended thus, not heard of after,
or met with others funnier, fouler, faster,
and were consumed, surviving as a chapter
meekly told
    in motley by a puppet,

while another fought each rival it encountered,
by quarries, caves, a peek through broken windows,
then a clamber through and dousing of all candles
for the pitch-black
    Bring it on – one filthy battle

all that story was. Others prospered
in the wishing-wells of luck where they were gathered
to remember, to remind and be reminded
All Tales Are True . . .
    so, when the mindless bandit

saw where they were hiding, they mistook it
for *An interesting new take on an old favourite*
and welcomed him with – you don't want to hear it –
the end is bones
    a-jingling in a market.

Stories grew like giants on the fats
of others, and they grew to stupid heights,
and they went to idiot lengths, and made great strides
while they could stand
     and a thousand and one nights

were all it took to winnow them to one.
And when it found us it eclipsed the sun.
Doffed its hat and started to sit down,
not obviously
     aware of our sign for pain

as it made itself at home. Now any story
but this was gone. It had digested stories
and some it had spewed out, it had spread stories,
poisoned them,
     but there were certain stories

had passed it by, like the story of the wind,
which, having no beginning and no end,
was not one, and was absent from its mind.
So, when, one day,
     wind came, when the ruined ground

rustled for it, when the brittle leaves
were stirring and the ash-white trees themselves
inhaled, inclined, when everything behaved
as if it lived
     again, as if it thrived,

the Story-of-All-Stories was afraid –
that a bigger one was coming, one that made
the picture move, the dead alive, the clouds
set out for somewhere
     without end or need,

and the Story-of-All-Stories cried the sound
of something shrinking to a cast of mind,
and then was blown to litter by the wind —
the bit you got's
    the bit that says THE END —

then the Story-of-All-Stories was gone.
— Deep in the library-stacks late afternoon,
you're that alone, the lights are bottle-green,
you sit there dazed
    your life went by again,

and you may well find yourself, in the way of dreams,
high on a ladder, straining towards the spines
for a battered book you lift down in your hands
and read elsewhere,
    and when you do you sense

a breeze as pages flicker to the end
or the beginning: you don't understand
a word. Let your tired face be fanned
by what the Story-
    of-All-Stories learned.

Fire Came

Fire came
    was the first line
of every story – it spread like story –
quicker, though,
so no one knew
the how or why while they were roaring

This is it!
    In the teeth of light
we made the changes creatures make
to appear strong
    or appear gone –
spines and antlers, slits of black,

fire-camouflage,
    heat-subterfuge,
feigning of death, feigning of terms –
Upon all fire
    we turn our fire
and we will seek it in two forms:

sunset –
    when it can't be yet –
savaging into our sights, or this soft
shape it takes:
    these cringing wicks,
shorn of their haloes, spat on, snuffed.

Rendition

It was quiet in their zone. They liked to call it
The Zone, it gave it borders.
But it gave the quiet an edge, it gave the quiet
a hum, more like a drone,

more like an engine coming through so they called it
Home. Then it went quiet.
Would you look at that, they said. They called all things
things that made them quiet.

They found a man so quiet what he knew
was everything there was to.
He was quiet when he was asked why was he quiet.
And he was asked why was he

LOUD when he was LOUD and he was LOUD
for 97 seconds.
Why are you loud, they said, you were so quiet.
He answered in both forms.

Why is it dark again, they said, it was light.
Why is there Guns N' Roses
playing, it was not. Why does this light-stick
leak, do you think it's busted?

The Switch

The quality of *mercy* being what it is,
I ran it by the group and it came back to me

in a clear plastic sleeve as the word *clemency*
with a jostling queue of question marks that grew in size

then forty bullet-points of his depravities
to expedite the process which indeed it has.

The Fool and She

She thought the fool a fool so she was in.
We noticed that she thought the fool a fool
when through the wailing fun
of the ragging we were doling out to the trapped fool
Is that arm yours? One pointed out
an arm too smooth for us and a wink of penknife.

I said I'd have a word. *It's just a game,*
mate, I confided, asked about her blade,
she went *Which one of them?*
Well all of them! – All afternoon I'm at her side,
calling the fool a fool again
as she spread the blades and told me to just pick.

She walked among us, always seemed to walk
between us, we weren't guards, that wasn't how
we needed it to look!
but she called the fool a fool in step *Let's do this now*
and everywhere we used to hope
the fool was there, we hoped he'd fucked off home.

But he wasn't anywhere, he was no fool.
We roam the splattered corridors, the only
sound in our old school
her coining us new names. We meet him only
in ballads of the several times
we've showed him, and will show all fools like him.

The Tinsel Man

What with the year we'd had it was in the air
to ditch that holiday but the thing is old,
    it's always held,
so it isn't up to us and to be fair
    the children like it.

So we prised the coffin-box and the cold breeze
was all our yesteryears, while on the road
    by the wayside
the man himself was spotted, his big face
    not understanding.

That days arrive as dates is not a thing
he gets, so to be hoisted shoulder-high
    hip hip hooray
and to be crowned with tinsel in the morning
    sunshine was something!

And we laughed into the town, at the great fools
we were again, and we took his weight in turns,
    we wrote new lines
for age-old melodies, we banged the bells
    in our tradition.

And he was fed before he had a chance
to ask to be, and had his pick of girls
    and was all smiles
but didn't pick and they just stroked his hands
    as he stared at us.

Who knows if he remembers this is what
we do with him? Who knows if he believes
    the town behaves
the same way every day? Who gives a shit
    is another thing.

And another thing is timing. It was noon,
then it was after noon, and the white sky
    so recently
blue in his brain was white so he gripped his throne
    and with his language

fought to stop it leaving him. His words
were belted out so loud they made one sound
    till that one sound
meant nothing. He was focused on some clouds,
    then other clouds.

Mime was all. We think what he meant was *Fight,*
They Are Everywhere, They Are Coming! But the sun
    blushed the maroon
the girls had worn and was gone from there. It was night
    and he didn't stop

wailing till the dawn came and the sun rose.
We leave him to his Morning Victory March
    to the near edge
of the wood as he sheds his terrible old clothes
    and decorations.

Old Smile at the Roast

Test for the Old Smile, they're going to roast it —
it'll have to keep its ends up all night,
for the secretary says she finds it creepy,
and the golfing partner says you got that right,

and the rival says it's fake, and the ambitious
junior makes his point with a few slides,
and the protégé the Smile was always sweet to
walks up and says it turns his insides.

They harp on it, the bosses and the buddies,
and things get even better by these lights,
which is to say it's shredded like a secret,
which is to say it's one of the great nights;

and folks are saying so while they're still roasting:
they cry out to the Smile and it smiles back,
like something huge is burdening a hammock,
or is until you hear a frightful crack. —

And then you better run like you saw nothing.
And then you better run like you weren't there.
There is a line, it's long and isn't smiling.
You won't believe me when I tell you where.

Catworld

And what you require attended to is always,
I notice, the one in the million-and-one things
I have to attend to, boon-companion
   in from the cold.

A bird or a mouse or a conglomeration of bird
and mouse with a wing of fur and a fan of bone
and its little eyelets of blood? You've done
   the old man proud.

Splendid. I am pleased with you, my only
pet. I agree that these once delicate things
lying in elongated chunks
   will do nicely.

I love you even more! I may not say it
for days on end, it could be our little secret,
but you know my every waking minute
   every thought

is of you, of your courage! While you sleep
and while I'm gone I'm boasting in the streets
until I'm hoarse about your exploits!
   Then they creep

towards me, every boy, and they come to rest,
every girl, and tuck their pretty wings
behind them. Every dog hangs
   from every lamp post.

Jones at Jonestown

On film his mouth is set, defiant, a fist,
any old tyrant's jaw at the end like any
brimming little boy's when it's all ruined
    and not his fault. The worst

that could have happened happened to his dream:
mums and dads and grown-ups in the background
beaming, trying to understand, but Jones
    is taking his toys home

if this goes on. Nine hundred smiley faces
all equal in the sight of him, all swept
from harm into a clearing, owing nothing,
    nine hundred old addresses

love reclaimed, love seeded into gardens –
and someone's pointing fingers? People have flown
from long ago to film this? Only the evil
    act like that. Their questions

stain the light. The fat sky drops to earth
fagged-out and sweating and its heat breaks loose
and frolics in the compound. There's an amp
    transmitting Jones's breath

and you can hear it catching on thorns,
squatting down to listen as some children
tell on him, and others tell on those ones.
    Then the breath coughs up guns

and the rain comes killing down as if one child
said to, said to get the mums and dads
all waiting on the airstrip, drenches them
    who shouldn't have grown old,

and now we can go on, the garden's ours,
and Jones is placing soldiers where he likes,
he's on all fours, rotating like a ride,
    so his big shoes like oars

are threshing what he put there till it's all
threshed and the bright future is restored.
Birds sing. The liquid's him if you love him,
    if you swallow it down whole.

The Execution of
St-Just at Thermidor

In his favourite coat, immaculately smart,
as if invited — as if death was *at home*
to him that day — he played a Frenchman's part

as everything went Roman. Robespierre,
who'd managed two whole letters of his name,
began to bleed to death with a frantic stare

while all the other suicides manqué
messily followed suit. But Louis Antoine
was beaming to himself as if to say

this too was written. Then he fixed his gaze
on the Declaration of the Rights of Man
where it hung like some old print from the old days,

and he said: *Well, we did that*. Sported a smile
at the barber's, in the carriage, on the stage,
in the spotlight, even afterwards a while.

Cassandra and the King

I can't remember if this happened yet
but the King came in and cleared out all his pals and sat
with everything akimbo and said *Do the bit
where I love you, little señorita, cut to it.*

So I told him what had happened, I mean hadn't yet,
and it was the longest time this man had ever sat
for anything. He roared *I now believe that bit!*
He wanted astonishment from me so I went for it.

I asked him if he'd got round to believing yet
that he'd be slaughtered where he stood. *Or where I sat?*
he chuckled, and I sat corrected. *Just a bit,*
he murmured, *I'm the King, of course I'll swing for it . . .*

But I'm going to free you, girl! I wouldn't do that yet,
I said, and someone came and served us as we sat
in lovely sunlight, then he dozed a little bit,
so I said Your wife will kill you. He said *Go for it*

mine angel. I do know, but didn't quite know yet
if that meant her or me. My little black cat sat
on Agamemnon's lap and bathed himself a bit.
She'll kill you in your bath. *Will you join me in it?*

he giggled. You will love me, sir, I said, and yet
you'll never have me. (This is the last time we sat
face to face.) 'Cause you won't get it up. He bit
his nails and stood. *You gypsy bitch you don't know shit.*

A Walk by the Neva

While the river gathers the many folds of its gown,
    rises to sit and turns to stone,
the figureheads
    on the rostral columns break out into brides

married in just a moment at the prow
    of Vasilyevsky Island. So
the city sails
    in time: the buildings glide in parallels,

the giant dreams his dreams of Holland. Peter's
    work is always done and never,
never quite,
    as another bridal party bustles into light

and the long white limos wait with their small bouquets,
    still as the marble case after case
of every tsar
    in the sharp fortress on the farther shore.

The widest flow flows to a point, and here
    there's you, in a crumpled suit somewhere,
picking me out
    of the line as a poet, there's you on a party night

with your beautiful new bride *This is my wife,*
    Mr Maxwell – the fact is, Joseph,
I didn't know,
    I thought you were having a laugh with a bloke and so

I stopped a waitress and said *By the way here's mine.*
There's a castle of drained pints in London
was it Highgate?
Hours of talk I don't forget and do forget,

as the widest flow flows to a point. And here
I am, where you are never. The air
flutters the last
bride of the morning. I am the Wedding Guest

at we all know which wedding, always about
to follow the congregation out
into sunlight,
but held by something at the garden gate

until the lawn's deserted and it's dark.
When will it ever be fucking dark
in the month of June
in this town of yours? Never, and pretty soon.

The limo driver's grinding a spotless shoe
on his dead cigarette and I knew you,
that's all.
The bride is impatiently at the beck and call

of a cameraman. The tiles of the river are old
snapshots, silver and brown and curled,
moving and still,
rustling into the east, into the equal.

Mandelstam

Knowing no word of his I embrace his every
word. They're all there is. He died for only
them. I imagine the obstinate syllables
of his name like a bothering hand on the lapels
of Stalin now and then. I imagine him
having it brushed away. Neither of them
strikes me as caring greatly about the dull
ache the other makes elsewhere in his skull,
not even when those closest to them come
wondering *What are you going to do about him?*

Only a slow accrual of discomfort
can do it, and only at night at a point where hurt
and thought converge and clarify the future
with nothing but new words, whether a line
begun forever or one jotted sentence.

All Things Bright

Long ago somewhere
he saw her first. He thought
with fists in pockets he might sidle there,
because it simply hurt
   to sit apart.

Sixty years that close
meant nothing much one night
by a garden lamp she wondered who he was.
He went to where she sat.
   Her eyes were bright

with nobody he knew.
He died inside a year.
They wheeled her chatting to her usual pew.
She wondered in mid-prayer
   why she was there,

and who we were nearby,
and why this awful hymn
All Things Bright they're singing now and why
would no one drive her home
   to lunch with him?

But our congregation sang,
as if we sang to drown –
with love of them – two lovers quarrelling,
who'd still be at it long
   after we'd gone.

Country Birthday

My special day was cold, empty and special.
I saw hardly anyone. I did all the things I wanted.
I had it from beautiful dawn to bitter old midnight.
Nothing was in it and everyone; I danced
to tracks on my own. The hours went out like mates.
I drank champagne and poured some more and began
talking. I took a few notes. It's the only day
I ever notice passing.
                              So it's the only
way I can get a sniff of the time it comes
sauntering into some cottage with a gift-box,
and it cries out loud *'Tis I!* then calls my name
without looking, then reads my post, then tramps upstairs
and peers in every room, and then, on the landing,
emits one puzzled *o . . . kay then*, before leaving.

Number Three

Three boys as in the story
are nothing till they're over the locked gate
to seek their fortunes. Somewhere in the bright
beyond there were these sisters . . .
    Which was so scary

we called them not by names
but numbers. Then again we were at war.
We were boys and they were girls so we had a war.
I remember Number Three
    at least in dreams

I do, I'm by their house:
I'm meant to attack in some way, both my hands
are paper-weighted with cold water-bombs
but I know I'm going to pay
    for all of this,

for I know I'm the second son
in the story, that I wind up in the end
spellbound and lumbering, all the numbers turned
to faces and me naked
    and forty-one.

Long Journey

Being too young to pass
the gate, we made our distance from a loop.
We'd ride around our house, and every lap
would be another mile
    into the mist.

Ten laps to France,
twenty there, a picnic in a field,
then twenty more to Germany, an old
box or two a Schloss
    by the back fence

and thirty more, who knows,
Austria, Russia . . . While my little brother
pedalled out of sight I'd fix a border:
a cold guard with a gun,
    a hostile pose,

harder questions. Eighty
laps away the world was very tense,
there were shots fired, he found me dead and once
I found him dead and once
    we separately

lay down and died.
Him in a heap by his bike in the back garden.
Me face-down in moss in the front garden.
Nothing happened for ages
    as our mum dried

the dishes at the sink,
and put them away and saw he was still there.
The clouds went slowly over Hertfordshire,
till the rain began to smudge
    the scarlet ink

of our cardboard Chinese flag.
But we stayed down in the drizzle, we were dead.
If the other had gone inside it was too bad.
He didn't cough. I didn't
    scratch my leg.

In distant lands we died
we were thinking as we trooped into the warm,
and washed our hands in water that was steam
in our own home with the day
    dark blue outside.

Lit Windows

When I go home again,
when I know so many homes, but I mean the home
with the longest vowel, when I wander the old realm,
I pass them on the lane,
   boys turned to men,

so I turn back to a boy
to pass them saying nothing. For it's death
to be where one is not, where every breath
is a heaving of the oars
   alone at sea.

I could grow white and old
and I will, I am well aware, grow white and old
looking through lit windows of the world
for people in their rooms;
   for the blue, cold

light of a TV on
in an empty room . . . girl at a light so bright
she's silhouette . . . a man who hangs his coat
and stands quite still . . . a mother
   agrees with someone

over cake . . . the frosted light
of suppertime, of bathtime, of sex.
I don't have what I have from reading books
but stopping by your homes
   to see these sights

and wondering forever
who is someone else? Who on earth
are all these people to have known this with,
this world? Whole skies of stars
   are a lesser wonder

than all your lights at evening,
all your lives. When the lights go out I'm there,
moving on. When it's dark the stars are clear,
their immaterial eyes
   believing, disbelieving.

Thinking: *Earth*

So I was thinking: *Earth*.
And I was earthed as any poet is
by the word alone in its own empty space.
Earth. How the word begins
    with force, as breath

begins and its vowel lasts
as dreams do – or the pauses between numbers –
for as long as the brain can take it. How it closes
as the tongue steps to the teeth,
    presses and rests

till the air is gone. *Earth*.
Seen only in its spot by pilots strapped
for oxygen, their exhalations trapped
inside a crystal ball,
    some ghost of myth

foreshadowed in a scribble
on a cave-wall. My garden's going south
by sixty miles a year, and the caught breath
of botanists – as strains
    mutate, redouble –

itself would power a mill
when they next breathe. Between twin hegemons
of ice and sand we wait, where the mindful seasons,
autumntime, springtime,
    lie down a while,

old exiled diplomats
whose answers were too intricate, too rich
for the liking of the tsar. Now on the edge
of deserts they endure
    odd tête-à-têtes.

    *

I fly above the earth
today, dreaming a moment when I'm old,
though living one undreamed-of as a child,
a sliver of pure luck,
    freedom, health,

statistically safe,
and yet aghast and tethered by the fibres
to everything. We'll chat to our dead forebears,
drawn to the life, on screens,
    soon enough.

On we fly until,
brilliant and sleepy between meals,
we come to land on islands green as apples.
We chat on the horizon's
    infinity-pool.

At night on jet-black screens,
if, as we slither back in our own choosing,
we accidentally click on Channel Nothing,
we might just spot through crackle
    of descending lines

what seems to be foul liquid
spreading over sand, but we're aware
was taken from ten miles in the air,
and is a million people
    run ragged.

        *

Earth. I have a daughter.
Heaven's what I say it is for her.
Telling her is all it is so far
for me. My only use
    for the word *forever*

is in those conversations.
Earth, I think we farmed that word from you
and now can't seem to make the damn thing grow
anywhere, for patience
    tries our patience.

That number on Times Square
plummets upward, digits to the right
are dim with speed. But the one on the far side
is locked at nil, as if
    it thinks we're there.

Graphs that all their lives
ran up and down like children now outreach
a lonely tentacle that leaves the page
to grope for something warm
    where nothing lives.

And it's been forty years,
eyeball to eyeball with the way we look,
blue and alone, bulb of a child awake,
wondering No, but *what's*
    behind the stars?

That casts me into space,
her father, the one opposite, old bloke
propped against a pillow on the dark,
helpless in the face of
    her helpless face,

while, home on earth again,
scientists are furrowing their brows
so deep they are thought mad by folk who raise
hosannas to the sky
    for Superman.

Hometown Mystery Cycle

for Claire Messud and James Wood

But I was one of the children told
they play the Creation on Applecroft Road
while Abel is battered on Barleycroft Lane
and if I go with him he'll cop it again

at the top of Old Drive. If I stay with the Ark
I'll have seen a good twenty-one Floods before dark,
but I know the place well as the front of my hand
so I watch it in zigzag and still understand.

The dawn's coming up over Handside Green
as Hell's being harrowed by Christ in sunscreen,
but another one rising by pulley-and-rope
at the corner of Mannicotts isn't the bloke

who Thomas is gaping at over his eggs
on a little white trestle on wobbly legs
by the scout hut on Guessens. The stone's rolled away
as slowly as you can roll papier-mâché,

and Judas is keeping his anorak zipped
as he checks on his lines in a ragged old script.
Pilate is bicycling by. If we're quick
we can leg it to Lazarus, set up our picnic,

still be in time for the beauty they've got to
assault with tomatoes till Jesus says not to.
Over the chimneys we hear as we hurry
the loudspeaker crackle the usual story

about a lost child, and we chuckle and say
You'll be late to an angel we pass on the way.
We hop all the hedges of Attimore Street,
where a girl who got rid of me rinses His feet,

and it's too much to take so I plod to the pool,
for the Slaughter of half my old nursery school,
but they lie there and giggle, they're clearly okay,
to the fury of someone who's *Herod today*

and gone tomorrow I joke to my mates
but they've spotted the Virgin in wraparound shades,
and we pass the Three Wise Men, muddled by props
in the shade of an alleyway down by the shops.

Afternoon tires of us, everyone tires;
I hang around people who hang around fires;
three mothers attempt to look vaguely surprised
He is striding already up Mandeville Rise;

but the little girl chosen Star-Girl for the day –
Has anyone seen her? – the drunken PA
is trying to be serious and nobody has.
The imbecile doing Balaam and his Ass

is playing for laughs so he's not getting any.
Judgment is here, they've unloaded already.
Satan is making a meal of a yawn.
We rush up to God *Hey we saw you at dawn!*

So how's the day been? and, to illustrate how,
He ploughs an old finger across an old brow
and puffs out His cheeks like we might blow away
but we don't understand so we nod and we stay;

we are gravely observing the fools in their cart,
then they go and it's quiet and He says *Can we start?*
to nobody really. Just one more to go,
but we've ticked every box so we've seen every show

and it's chaos again as it is every year
with the carts in a ditch and *Whose bloody idea*
was this in the first place? somebody bawls
in the queue for the luminous-necklace stalls,

but he can't really mean it, he has paper wings
that his daughters deface with embarrassing things;
he's played about every last role in the Cycle
(he'd never been Michael but now he's been Michael)

and someone is holding a ladder that trembles
and someone has wound a great zero of cables
around his strong arm, and he stares in my eyes
as I say *Weren't you Peter?* which yes he denies

and someone is binding the Cross to a Jeep
and someone is bearing a burden asleep
with a garland of foil and a cellophane star,
who, in other versions, is found in a bar

and in at least one is found stabbed in a pit.
You know your own villages: write your own shit.
I've never done much and I didn't do this,
but you asked where I come from and that's where it is.

Blues for Cassie

Woke up as lonesome as the one dead
    white guy in that flood
who edged into the frame
    on primetime.
Folk said *Baby look look look*
    he can't be I mean fuck.
The station was just inund . . .
    never mind.

Woke up as lonesome as the single
    snapshot at Grand Central –
of thousands on a wall
    one endless fall –
of someone who turned up again
    alive, the one
straw in all them landfills
    of needles.

Woke up as lonesome as somebody
    gone whose one and only
trace you're gawping at,
    lil' shipmate.
Turn off the news, pass by the wall,
    flip this page and we'll
be done so I don't see
    ya dump me.

Cassandra by the Wall

Fire came and went and soon. In my gripped eyes
you soothe. You see twin flames
and shush them. When it comes your open eyes
will show a crow's-eye view:
twin turrets burning with the eyeballs murders.

It was long ago; it was yesterday; next Wednesday.
Guess which cup. You found me
resting by my wall on one of my good days,
eyes lowered and watching it
happen before in the sand, happen in ant-world.

I don't even mention this in my mad politeness.
I loom my face so close
to all of you great laughter is occasioned,
like when I said your world
would end up as a crayoning-book for children.

Cassandra

You. I won't foresee for you one thing.
You staring into space, you moulding creatures.

You thinking if you stop it then the world ends.
Little old you, it does. Mine doesn't, yours will.

But I won't foresee for you, you won't believe me.
You rub your eyes and write. You've not believed

life's anything but a grin into the mist
for some time now, although you gasp at line-breaks

like something spoke to you. O it spoke to you.
I'm at your window now: I breathe the year

you'll leave on the warm glass. Beyond my wild hair
blossoms the to-come but you're so distracted,

you, by my lips, my ways, you think like me –
wake with one face a sniff away forever,

speak the lines she speaks at the moment she
speaks these you speak and set your lips where she does,

then you'll see nothing coming or becoming,
and all will be so well. – It will be well,

but I won't let you hear that. If you hear it
you won't believe it, there's where our curses meet

like kisses. All will be well. You didn't hear it,
you, therefore believe it, as your fingers

whittle at the keys to the bright screen,
as the windowpane goes cold and I move on,

trespassing away down your lawn,
over the wall and out across farmland.